MELAN(
MOME

AND

RANDOM THOUGHTS

POEMS OF REFLECTION

MELANCHOLY MOMENTS

AND

RANDOM THOUGHTS

POEMS REFLECTING THE LOSS OF A CHILD AND LIFE IN GENERAL

ANNE SEDDON

P.A.M.S. Books

First published in 2005 by:
P.A.M.S. Books
53 Front Street
Seaton Burn
Newcastle On Tyne
NE13 6EP

ISBN: 0-9549502-0-8

Printed and bound in Great Britain by:
ProPrint, Riverside Cottages, Old Great North Road, Stibbington, Cambridgeshire PE8 6LR

Cover designed by Anne Seddon.

FOREWORD

I have always loved poetry. It is something that has poured out of me, usually during the hardest moments of my life. 'Twas at such a time that Anne began writing hers, her therapy to cope with the untimely loss of her wonderful son.
It is my belief that he is now enjoying a new and incredible adventure elsewhere. Yet Anne has begun her own quest to share all of her emotions, peaks, troughs, pleasures and pains with us.
I don't care that it is not sophisticated or intellectually challenging because it is from the heart, and that really is all that counts.
It is my honour to play a tiny part in the rebuilding of Anne Seddon. She is great and I hope this book will begin a new chapter in her life.

Love and Blessings

Alan Robson M B E

ACKNOWLEDGEMENTS

My grateful thanks to Alan Robson
and all the Night Owls
for helping me through many a long and lonely night

And

My thanks to Ramon
for his patience in teaching me that a computer will not
blow up when I switch it on.

INTRODUCTION

I wrote these poems randomly – on a bus –
At work – in the middle of the night –
Anywhere in fact – as a way of releasing the
pain of losing my child.
I could not understand the mixture of emotions that swept
over me
changing so rapidly Anger, disbelief, denial, pain, tears,
hysterical laughter, sometimes all rolling into one.
Putting on a brave face for the outside world
Whilst crumbling up inside.
I hope that by reading these poems
others who have suffered such a loss and have gone through or
are still going through this variety of feelings will realise they are
not going mad but that these feelings are perfectly natural and
that they are not isolated as many thousands of people will be
sharing the same thoughts and emotions.

The second part of this book contains
feelings and thoughts of a wider nature.

This book is dedicated to my two sons

Stephen and Mark
To thank them
for all their love and support
throughout the years

And *is in memory of my son Paul*
Born 1959
Died at the age of 25 years on

May 31st 1985

Contents Part One

MELANCHOLY MOMENTS

*We should cherish and protect
our children
as we do not know how long
they will be in our lives*

TWENTY YEARS AGO

Twenty years ago today
God took my darling son away
He went away without a sign
I'll miss him till the end of time.

They say time heals, but still today
This burning pain won't go away.
They say time heals, but that's not true
I never will get over you.

They say time heals, but I can't explain
This emptiness, this endless pain.
You were my life, my pride, my joy,
My first born son, my darling boy.

Anne Seddon

For Paul's 20th Anniversary May 31 2005

IN MY ARMS

When you were placed into my arms
My heart just filled with pride!
I felt a surge of warmth and love
That came from deep inside.

My firstborn child my darling son
You brought with you such joy
From that first day we were as one
Light of my life – my darling boy.

Anne Seddon

WHEN YOU WERE BORN

When you were born I did not know
You were not mine to keep
God only lent you to me
Till He said you should sleep.

He said that you were needed
In that place up in the sky
He did not give me any choice
Or give a reason why.

God just said 'Thank you
'For looking after Paul for me,
But my need for him is greater
You must now set him free.'

Anne Seddon

THROUGH THE MIST

Through the mist of my dreams I still see your face,
The love in your eyes no time can erase.

Your arms are outstretched, your breath in the air,
I reach out and feel the silk of your hair.

I know you're not real, I know you are dead,
But your vision is clear, it won't leave my head.

I'm happy I dream and your love I can keep,
You're with me awake, and you're with me asleep.

The memories of you go round in my head,
Why did God take you and not me instead?

I love you so much I can't set you free,
The memories I have, just won't let me be.

I wonder around see you in a trance,
Sometimes in full view, sometimes just a glance.

I miss you so much, and I can't let you go,
How can life go on? I really don't know.

One day we will be together again,
I'll just have to dream about you until then.

The light of my life my pride and my joy,
My wonderful – handsome – my own darling boy!

Anne Seddon

MY WEE LAD!

Anyone who's lost a child
Will know just how I feel!

This pain, this hurt, this emptiness,
This blow from which I reel!

Life has dealt a lot of blows,
That made me truly sad,

But nothing else can equal
The loss of my wee lad!

Anne Seddon

IF I CLOSE MY EYES

I close my eyes and yet I see
A thousand 'Pauls' surrounding me.
I touch his face and stroke his hair
His wondrous voice just fills the air.

I feel his arms around me tight
He whispers 'Mam I'll be alright'
He wraps me up and holds me near
Saying 'I'm with God so have no fear.'

'Cry not for me and don't be sad,
For now I'm safe you should be glad.
I'm happy now in Heaven, though I did not want to go,
It's peaceful here with angels although I still miss you so.'

'I'm safe in the hands of Jesus
And he is looking after me
So Mam be strong and brave
And set my spirit free.'

So Paul my son I hear you
And I'm really going to try
To leave you in the care of God
And try hard not to cry.

Anne Seddon

MY BEAUTIFUL SON

My beautiful son where are you?
Why did you have to go?
My beautiful son I need you!
You must know I love you so!

My beautiful son I miss you!
Why was there no goodbye?
My beautiful son I ache for you!
You must know how I cry?

My beautiful son God called for you!
He gave no reason why!
My beautiful son I pray for you!
Why did you have to die?

My beautiful son I long for you!
But I know you are at rest!
My beautiful son be peaceful now!
God only takes the best!

Anne Seddon

OH! PAUL!

Oh! Paul my son where are you
Why have you gone away?
When I gave birth to you my son
I thought you were here to stay.

God gave three precious gifts to me
To last my whole life through
Why did he take one back again?
And leave me with just two.

God gave three precious sons to me
I thought were mine to keep
Yet now just two are wide awake
And one is fast asleep.

But God decided different
He said we had to part
But he just did not take my son

He took my very heart!

Anne Seddon

PAUL

My darling how I miss you
No one will ever know.
This pain inside my breaking heart
Just seems to grow and grow.

No time to say 'I love you'
No time to say 'Goodbye'
You left us oh! So suddenly
And gave no reason why.

If I could have any wish today,
I'd ask for only one.
That the Lord would open up his arms
And give me back my son.

We love and miss you Paul.

Anne Seddon

IT SEEMS LIKE ONLY YESTERDAY

It seems like only yesterday
They said that you were dead
I cannot stop those dreadful words
From pounding in my head.

I cannot ever come to terms
With losing you my son.
For you were such a young man,
And your life had just begun.

You were thoughtful and so loving
So strong yet gentle too
I never have felt whole again
Since the day that I lost you!

Anne Seddon

MY SON

I once had a son who sparkled with love
And shone with a glow that came from above.
I once had a son who possessed the power
To bring out the sun in the midst of a shower.

Now you have gone son,
And with you my love,
Nothing but darkness falls from above.

The sun's no longer shining,
The sky no longer blue,
My life has no meaning my son without you.

Anne Seddon

WHAT IS THIS LIFE?

What is this life so full of pain
That knows no sun but only rain?
No sleep by night no rest by day
Can nothing take this pain away?

My heart is broken, inside I cry
Why did my darling son have to die?
My body's numb I cannot feel
These nightmare thoughts cannot be real.

Anne Seddon

IT CAN'T BE TRUE

I can't explain the way I feel
It can't be true, it can't be real.
An empty room, an empty chair,
And yet I see you sitting there!

Can this be right?
This thing they say?
That you will not be home today!

You called my name
I was not there,
Your dying breath I did not share.
My darling son what can I do
To make things right again for you?

When God decided you must go
Did he not know I need you so?
I love you so, I can't explain
How much I need you back again.

You're part of me
My darling boy
My firstborn son – my pride – my joy.

It can't be true – you can't be dead!
You must be fast asleep in bed!

I cannot tell, I can't explain
This living hell!
This burning pain!

Anne Seddon

MY CHILD

My heart it aches with loneliness
Because you've gone away
My arms they ache with emptiness
And that's the way they'll stay.

I miss your laugh I miss your smile,
I miss your cheeky face
If I live to be a hundred
No one can take your place.

Anne Seddon

DON'T WANT TO GET UP

Don't want to get up in the morning
Can't fall asleep at night
Don't know what is going on inside my head
But something isn't right.

I feel my life is over
No use to anyone.
No happiness in living
An effort to carry on.

I cannot work – there's too much pain
Just feel redundant once again.
This empty feeling every day
Since God took my darling son away.

I try so hard no one can see
This gaping hole inside of me
I'd love to wake up with a feeling of joy

But that cannot happen without my wee boy!

Anne Seddon

CAN ANYBODY UNDERSTAND?

Can anybody understand
The feelings that I hide?

The loneliness and heartache
That I keep locked up inside?

The pain, the hurt, the misery,
This hole that's never filled.

The loss, the stress, the hopelessness
Since the day my son was killed?

I must be a worthless person
For God to hurt me so.

They say that time will ease the pain
But to me it seems to grow.

I try to get through daily life,
And take things day by day

They all say soon this pain will cease
But *I know it's here to stay!*

Anne Seddon

WHEN WILL I?

When will I ever be whole again?
When will I feel fulfilled?
Two children now have left the home
Another one was killed.

When will I ever feel happy again?
When will I start to smile?
When will life feel good again?
And each day not a trial?

When will I ever be needed again?
And not be obsolete?
When will my children come home again –
To make my life complete?

Anne Seddon

PAUL'S BIRTHDAY

That very special day
Is always in my heart
God gave you to me for a while
Too soon we had to part.

I bless the day forever
That God gave you to me
My heart was filled with love and pride
For all the world to see

All too soon your life was over,
No birthdays any more!
Too soon God took away – the son that I adore.

Anne Seddon

BIRTHDAY MEMORIES

Oh! Jesus, give my darling son
A very special day
Look after him and love him,
And protect him all the way.

For he is a special person,
The best that there could be,
And he really should be spending
His birthday here with me!

We love and miss you.

Anne Seddon

MY SONS

My three boys are all so different
That anyone can see

The only thing they have in common
Is they all are part of me!

Anne Seddon

GOD'S GIFTS

In this long unhappy life
God gave three gifts to me
Three sons so good and wonderful
They mean the world to me.

Each of them is special
In their unique and caring way
Each of them renewed my strength
To cope from day to day.

Then for some obscure reason
God took one son from me!
He never did explain it
Nor try to help me see.

Now my two sons they try so hard
Their brother's place to fill
But no matter just how hard they try
I know they never will.

For part of me is missing,
Yes part of me is dead.
God could easily have taken me
Why take my son instead?

My two sons still are special
In their unique and caring way
But their brother he is missing
And lost along the way.

Anne Seddon

PRECIOUS GIFTS

God gave three precious gifts to me
That filled my heart with love,
Three sons to love and cherish
For whom I thank the Lord above.

My first son's name is Paul
So gentle and so kind
Somebody quite as generous
Would be very hard to find.

My middle son is Stephen
So chatty and so loud,
His kindness and his caring
Make him stand out in a crowd.

My youngest son is Mark
As quiet as can be
Intelligent and caring
For all the world to see.

How come each one is different?
It's really baffling you see
And yet one thing I'm proud of is –
They all belong to me!

However will they all grow up?
Whatever will they be?
It doesn't really matter
They are all the world to me!

Anne Seddon

WHERE ARE YOU?

Where are you now my first born?
Why have you gone away?

When Jesus gave you to me
I thought you were here to stay.

What will I do without you?
Now that I'm on my own.

I never thought you'd leave me
Broken hearted and alone.

Anne Seddon

IF ONLY

If only I had listened
To what you had to say.
If only I had been with you
On that awful, fateful day
To guide you and protect you
Your problems son to share!
I really feel I failed you
Because I was not there.

If only I had loved you more!
Or maybe loved you less!
Would anything have changed things?
I can only really guess.

Anne Seddon

THE EARLY HOURS

In the early hours of the morning
I waken up and pray
That when the new day's dawning
You will be home to stay.

I know that is impossible
I know you never will,
And yet on every single day
I wake up – hoping still!

I find it very difficult
To accept that you are gone
I try to think up reasons
And yet – I know that there are none.

Anne Seddon

ON LOAN

God lent you to me for a while
With trusting eyes
And wistful smile.

You filled my heart with wondrous love
My special gift, from up above.

I needed you in every way
I never thought you'd go away.

But when he called you had to go
From all of us who love you so.

Anne Seddon

THE QUIET OF THE NIGHT

Two o'clock in the morning
The worst time of the day
When all the fears and loneliness
Come flooding back to stay.

The house is oh so quiet,
The whole world seems asleep,
I walk around in deep despair
In – pain – alone I weep!

Whatever happened to the life
I worked hard to achieve?
What happened to my family?
Why did they have to leave?

Why am I in this empty place?
This house that's not a home
Why did God take you all from me,
And leave me all alone?

Anne Seddon

IMAGINE!

Imagine life that has no sun
That has no day just night!
Imagine life where no one laughs
Where all they do is fight!

Imagine life that has no warmth
That's always wet and cold!
Imagine life where no one's young
Where everybody's old!

Imagine life that's dull and drab
Where everything's a chore!
Imagine life without a song
Where everyone's at war!

I don't have to imagine
For me that life is real
Since my son died – no happiness
Just pain inside I feel.

The days are dark and lonely
The night times never end
I've lost touch with reality
And with all my friends

For no one else can understand the pain that I go through
Each second and each minute since the day that I lost you!

Anne Seddon

MY LOVELY CAT

On the day God took my son from me
He sent something in his place
A lovely little kitten
With the cutest little face.

He slept alongside me at night
And followed me by day.
He never let me out of sight
Saying 'Mum I'm here to stay.'

He loved me and he cuddled me
And never left my side
He licked the teardrops from my face
Every single time I cried.

He tried his very best to help
He knew my every mood
He always read my mind you see
He truly understood!

He placed his paws around me
Snuggled close against my face
He tried so hard to comfort me
My sadness to erase.

Anne Seddon

MY CAT

My darling Tips the day you came
My heart was split in two
You see God took away my son
The day that he sent you!

You came to me with all your love
And helped me through the pain
You helped me out for quite a while
Till God took you also back again.

Anne Seddon

LOST

The sound of the sea and the wind and the surf
Are pounding around in my head!

I can't understand what is happening to me
I'm filled with such fear and such dread.

The future is misty, the past is a blur
I really don't know what to do!
I ache for you, long for you
Yet somehow I know
I never again will see you!

I feel you caress me
Although you're not here,
I feel your soft kiss on my cheek.
I must find you soon, or I cannot go on
You're just like a drug that I seek.

I'm lost and alone and I can't find my way
It seems like my life is a maze
I call for you, reach for you ,
Yet deep down I know
You're lost in the fog and the haze.

Anne Seddon

YOUR VISION

I gazed into the night and there you were!
You came into my sight,
Without a stir.

I'd thought of you each night
And of the way you held me tight
That there you were
Yes there you were
In sight!

You stood against the sky
For quite a while
Arms outstretched to me
You gave a smile

I'd thought so much of you
And of the things we used to do
That there you were, yes there you were
In view.

I closed my eyes and prayed
That you would stay.
But when I looked again,
You'd gone away.

Your vision it had gone
But your memory lingers on
And you are here
Yes you are here in my heart.

Your vision was so clear
And you seemed so very near
That you were there,
Yes you were there in view.

Anne Seddon

I'M TIRED

I'm tired of waking up with my stomach on the floor,
Desperately waiting for my son to walk back through the door

I can't believe I'll never see his smiling face again,
One day we'll be reunited, but only God knows when!

Each day seems like a lifetime, the minutes pass so slow,
The way I ache – and – weep – and sob, no one will ever know!

I'm tired of waking up with my stomach on the floor,
So desperately unhappy – I cannot take much more.

I hardly ever sleep at night and even when I do
My dreams are full of loneliness, because my son I have lost you!

I keep this pain deep down inside, pretending to be fine,
Somehow I've got to hide this hurt – for these other sons of mine.

Anne Seddon

WHEN AM I GOING TO DIE?

When am I going to die?
How long do I have to wait?
How come nobody ever knows
What's going to be their fate?

Don't want to get up in the morning,
Can't fall asleep at night,
Don't know what's going on inside my head
But something isn't right!

I feel my life is over,
No more use to anyone,
No happiness in living,
An effort to carry on.

I cannot work – there's too much pain
Just feel redundant once again.
This empty feeling every day
Since God took my darling son away.

I try so hard! No one can see
This gaping hole inside of me.
I'd love to wake up with a feeling of joy,
But that cannot happen without my dear boy!

Anne Seddon

I DON'T KNOW HOW!

I don't know how to cope with these feelings inside
I really have worked, and I really have tried!
There's nobody left to love and to care,
Nobody around me these feelings to share!

I'm hurting so badly don't know what to do,
How do I manage my sons without you?

No longer I'm needed, you've lives of your own,
My life is so empty without you at home.

I miss all the noise, the tears and the joys,
This home's just a house, without my three boys.

What can I do to make you all see
This motherly love that's trapped inside me!

Anne Seddon

FOR TWO SPECIAL PEOPLE

There is someone here who loves you
Much more than words can say
There is someone here who misses you
And aches for you each day.

There is someone here who'd die for you
And who longs to hold you tight!
There is someone here who prays for you
And cries for you each night.

Your daddy was my little boy
And he meant the world to me
And when he died it broke my heart
But my darlings can't you see?

He left you here, his pride and joy,
His lovely girl, his handsome boy!
He left you here to take his place
You had his name, you had his face!

He loved you both so very much
You filled his heart with love
And I know that he is watching you
From his new home high above.

Yet someone in your tender lives
Turned you away from me.
But some day you will realise
Yes some day you will see –
That a Nana's love is special,
A Nana's love is real
And no matter what is said or done
No one can change the way I feel!

Anne Seddon

I STILL BELIEVE IN GOD!

I still believe in God!
Why does he not believe in me?
He never listens to my prayers
My pain he does not see.

No matter what I pray for
No matter what I need
No matter just how hard I try
I never can succeed.

I only want a happy home
With someone who truly cares
But I have searched and I have tried
But never have I found the answer to my prayers.

Oh! God please listen to my prayer
Don't turn your back on me!
For I have sinned and now I'm lost
And I need your help you see!

I need to feel somebody's arms
Enfold me close with love
If I can't find that one on Earth
Please hold me from above.

Anne Seddon

MISTAKES

Many mistakes I have made in my life
As a daughter a mother a friend and a wife.

I've tried far too hard to get everything right,
That of important things, I've sometimes lost sight.

I wanted my children to be honest and true,
So I was too strict in what they could do.

I kept too tight a rein so they would not stray,
And restricted their movements day after day.

But even though I've been ever so tough,
They have all taken the smooth with the rough.

They know what I did was meant for the best
And with flying colours they sailed through the test.

And although I know I got many things wrong,
They know that my love is undying and strong.

They are loving and caring and so full of love
They are really a blessing from Heaven above.

Anne Seddon

HELP ME GOD!

Oh! God help me carry on along life's rugged way,
Oh! God help me to be strong, to face each lonely day.
Oh! God help me not to sin, to make no more mistakes,
Oh! God help me to be good, no matter what it takes.

Oh! God I've done a lot of things, of which I am not proud,
Oh! God I've said so many things that should not have been allowed!
Oh! God I'm only human, bad things I've done a few,
Oh! God please forgive me, and let me start anew!

Oh! God help me to understand the crazy things I do
Oh! God help me live each day! A little more like you!

Anne Seddon

I DIE A LITTLE

I die a little every day
I just can't chase these blues away
My world is turning upside down,
I never smile, I only frown.

I hurt in every single way,
This pain is surely here to stay.
My life means nothing any more,
Since the day you walked out of that door!

I only know I must be strong,
And try my best to get along!
Why did you ever have to go?
Why did you have to hurt me so?

Anne Seddon

AS I WALK

As I walk along the windswept shore
And gaze out to the sea,
I wonder what else life has in store
For a lonely soul like me!

My life is cold and empty
And all I feel is fear and pain,
And I wonder if I ever will
Feel happiness again?

Anne Seddon

NOBODY HEARS ME

Nobody hears me crying, nobody feels my pain,
Nobody knows just how I feel
Now that I'm alone again.

Nobody hears me sobbing, nobody sees the tears,
Nobody feels me aching
Or understands my fears.

Nobody sees me walk the floors
Throughout the lonely night,
Nobody to help and comfort me
Nobody to hold me tight.

I stumble through the daytime
Not knowing what to do,
Then walk the floors throughout the night
Crying endlessly for you.

I know no one can help me
Get rid of all this pain,
I know no one can ever
Bring you back to me again.

Anne Seddon

THE END!

The waves crashed and played
With the rocks down below

The wind surged so fierce and so strong
My head and my heart pounded,

Oh where did you go?
What happened? Where did it go wrong?

I love you! I need you!
I can't stand this pain

I need your arms round me once more!

My tears tumble down as they mingle with rain,

One leap I could crash to the shore
But somehow I know that I must go on and face life
With courage and pride

For one son may have been taken from me
But two more are still at my side.

Anne Seddon

Contents

Part Two – RANDOM THOUGHTS

Late at night,
When the house is empty
And I feel so all alone
All I have to do
Is press a button
And suddenly
The house is bursting at the seams
With all my Night Owl friends

WHAT'S HAPPENED TO?

What's happened to this world of ours
Where has it all gone wrong?
Why is there all this hate and war,
Why can't people get along?

The fighting and the bombing
The hatred and the pain
When will people get along
And live in peace again?

I'm frightened for the future
And where it all will end
If they don't stop this hatred
And change enemy to friend.

I'm frightened for our children
If we don't learn to care
If we don't learn to love again
And this world of ours to share

So come on everybody
Let's each one do our share
To make this whole world safe again
Filled with love and filled with care.

Anne Seddon

IF I COULD TURN THE CLOCK BACK

If I could turn the clock back
I only wish I could!
There are lots of things I wouldn't do
And lots of things I would!

If I could turn the clock back
There are a lot of things I'd change
Yes lots of things I'd alter
Wipe out – or re-arrange.

If I could turn the clock back
And start my life anew,
I'd wipe out all of my mistakes
Yes! That's just what I'd do!

We only have one chance at life
And I've made a mess of mine
So if I could turn the clock back
Then that would be just fine.

Because I cannot turn the clock back
And can't undo the mess I've made
Then I must live with everything
And count the price I've paid.

Anne Seddon

WHY?

Why is life so cruel?
Why does it cause such pain?
Why does it want to hurt me
Time and time again?

From being such a small child,
To being old and grey,
The pain keeps on repeating,
And never goes away.

A childhood that was lonely,
That felt so cold and bare.
Nobody's arms to comfort me
No loving words to share.

Growing up so lonely,
So lost and so forlorn,
The only time that I felt love,
Was when my sons were born.

Why is life so cruel?
Why do I feel so sad?
Why do people use me?
And make me feel so bad?

No reason to get up in the morning,
Too frightened to go to sleep!
No reason to burst out laughing
But every reason to weep!

Anne Seddon

WHAT IS WRONG WITH ME?

I wake up frightened in the night
No one to comfort me
Nobody's arms to hold me tight,
No one for company!

I feel so cold and empty,
So lost and so alone,
No one to share my life with
Forever on my own.

Why am I always second best?
Why does no one put me first?
For no one to really love me
I really must be cursed!

I need someone to hold me
To keep me safe and warm,
Someone to keep my fears at bay,
To keep me from all harm.

I've so much love to offer,
So God how can it be?
There's no one close beside me
To give some love to me?

No one to say 'I love you'
No one to say 'I care'
I look towards my husband,
But he is no longer there!

Anne Seddon

WHAT IS LOVE?

What is love? I do not know!
They say it fills you with a glow
What is love? Where can it be?
It certainly has not come to me!

What is love? Is it around?
Can you tell me where it's found?
What is love? I wish I knew!
They say it comes to quite a few.

What is love? I'd like to try!
They say it makes you laugh and cry.
What is love? How can it be –
It comes to most but never me?

What is love? Is it so rare
That no one with me wants to share?
What is love? Where can it be?
Why does it hide from only me!

Anne Seddon

BE STRONG

The wind and the rain and the sea and the sand
All merge just as night into day.

Where are you my darling? I hear myself call
As I run getting soaked from the spray.

I know life is tough and you feel you must go
But darling don't end it this way.

Be strong trust in me
And together you'll see
We will fight through the fear and the pain.

At last oh my love, you are safe in my arms
Though you're
Cold, full of fear and in pain.

But now that I've snatched you away from the sea
I won't let you leave me again.

Be strong, trust in me
Together you'll see

We will fight all the illness and pain.

Anne Seddon

CRY NOT MY SONS

Cry not my sons!
Because I'm gone!
My heart is still with you!

Grieve not my sons!
Though I'm not there!
For I'm so proud of you!

Be brave my sons!
And carry on
The way I want you to!

Be strong my sons!
And stride along!
With hearts so kind and true!

Stand firm my sons!
And do not sway,
And I will walk with you!

My pride, my joys
My sons, my boys.

I always will love you!

Anne Seddon

DESCRIPTION OF ME

Can anybody realise the pain that's in my heart?
This feeling of rejection that has been with me
From the start?
Nobody's love to comfort me, a father who is dead
This aching through my body, this pounding
Through my head.

Why does my life seem different from everyone I know?
Why do I worry all the time
And not go with the flow?

I feel I'm on the outside, always looking in
I feel I can't be happy as that would be a sin!

For every time I start to laugh,
Something else in life goes wrong
Yes every time I start to smile
Another heartache comes along!

Why am I so obsessed with death?
Why does it fill my mind?
Why does it make me catch my breath
With reasons I can't find!

When I had my children I worried every day
If I was to die and leave them,
Where would they go to stay?
Nobody ever offered to look after them for me
Nobody saw the panic that filled the whole of me.

Why do I go on living when I really want to die?
Why pretend that I am happy,
When that really is a lie!
Why does nobody listen when I say how much I hurt?
Why put me down and criticise and treat me just like dirt!

Do they know how hard it is to get up and face each day?
To only watch and listen, and never have a say?
I feel just like a nobody, that no one seems to see
I only hope that no one else feels unhappiness like me!

I cannot take my own life cannot end the pain you see
For I cannot do to others, what has been done to me!
Still I must try to carry on and do the best I can
To cope with all this misery since this lonely life began!

I need someone to hold me and keep me free from harm
To love me and protect me and to change this fear to calm!

Anne Seddon

60 YEARS TOGETHER

60 years together, can it really be that long?
Since the two of you were married
And heard that wedding song?

60 years together each one better than the last,
You really have been lucky,
When you look into the past.

Like every other couple you've had your ups and downs
But because you love each other
There have been more laughs than frowns.

You are friends and true companions, and yes you're lovers too,
You never did regret the day, you smiled and said '*I do*'

You love each other now, even more than you did then,
And given even half a chance
You'd do it all again.

You are bound with love together your two hearts they entwine
And that's the way it will go on until the end of time.

So may you now look forward to many happy years
For as long as you're together
Life will hold no fears.

Anne Seddon

OH! TO BE YOUNG AGAIN!

Oh! What I'd give to walk down the street
With a swing of the hips and a skip of the feet!
To run for a bus or dance round the floor
Or run down the stairs to answer the door.

What is this old age that comes to us all,
That slows us all down turning run into crawl!
It creeps up unseen with never a glance!
It changes our lives we don't stand a chance!

I envy the young who do all these things!
Who fly all around as though they had wings!
And yet they don't know as they laugh and they sing
What comes to us all –
What a few years will bring!

Anne Seddon

HOW CAN YOU?

How can you say you love me?
How can you say you care?
When every time I turn around
I look! And you're not there!

You're at the pub or at the match
Or at the betting shop!
You're down the road or with your mates
The list will never stop!

I think you're there, but then you're gone
Just like a puff of smoke!
I seek you here I seek you there
It's really just a joke!

You could be in the garden shed
Or in your pigeon coo
You could be tucked up snug in bed
Or sitting on the loo!

One thing I know for certain!
I know you're not with me!
And yet you say you love me!
I know that cannot be!

Anne Seddon

FYBROMYALGIA

If I had an illness that everyone could see
They'd bring me chocs and flowers and numerous cups of tea!
If I had an illness that made me lose some weight
They'd give me lots of sympathy and want to be my mate!
If I had an illness that really was well known
They all would come and visit me and never leave me
on my own.

But because FM is unheard of, and because I'm getting fat!
Nobody ever listens – nobody gives a bat!
Because I look so healthy and keep a smile upon my face
They sometimes can get ratty when I cannot stand the pace!

I'm tired of people thinking I've gone lazy and so slow,
How much I want to work again, no one will ever know!
I'm tired of people thinking I must be eating like a pig
Will they never understand that FM makes you big!

No one can see this pain I'm in, the hopelessness I feel
When will the whole world recognise

That FM it is real!

Anne Seddon

VALENTINE FOR A NEW LOVE

Although I haven't known you long
I feel that you're the best
And yet I know I could be wrong
You could be like the rest!

Time will tell exactly
Yes in time we'll really see
You'll either love me and protect me
Or you'll walk away from me.

Anne Seddon

LOST LOVE

We'll never be together
But I've loved you from the start
I'll always keep a place for you
Here safe within my heart.

I hope that you'll be happy
Whatever you may do
Deep down I know you love me
And you know that I love you.

Anne Seddon

NEW LOVE

Don't let any new love ever tell you what to do,
Don't let any new love change you from being you!

Don't let any new love rake into the past
You both must keep your freedom
If you want new love to last

Share lots of things together
Yet still have room to breathe
Never give into threats of 'Do what I say or leave!'

You've had your share of heartache, so now you need a life
That's full of love and understanding, and never full of strife!

If someone says they cannot manage if you ever go away
Remember that is no reason
To feel that you should stay!

So please think things through carefully,
Try to make no more mistakes,
Think long and hard before you jump!
For everybody's sake.

It's better to live life alone if things are not quite true
Than to share your life with someone
Who is waiting to rule you!

Anne Seddon

WHY?

I was content in all my solitude
Until the day you came my way
Till gradually I fell in love
A little more each day.

I tried hard not to fall in love
Yet it happened anyway
The feelings that I had for you
Grew stronger every day.

You told me that you loved me too
And that you hoped we'd never part
And yet now I have discovered
You were just playing with my heart.

Why did God let this happen
Why does he pick on me?
Why not pick on someone stronger
Who does not hurt so easily?

I guess he has his reasons
I only wish I knew
Why he gives a glimpse of happiness
Then hurts me all anew!

Anne Seddon

REMEMBERING

I'm lying here remembering
The things you used to say
The way you said you'd love me
Forever and a day.

You said you'd never ever known
Such happiness before
And that with every breath you took
You loved me more and more.

You said you'd love and cherish me
And take me for your wife
And that for you I'd always be
The most important thing in life.

Anne Seddon

THE PAST

Why am I so lonely? Why am I so blue?
It's because I do not want to live
My darling without you.

I close my eyes and curl up tight
And hope I will sleep through the night.

I toss and turn and try to sleep
But all I do is sob and weep.

The bed seems cold and empty
The night so dark and still
I long to feel you next to me
But I know I never will.

I tried to make you happy
And do everything for you
If you live to be a hundred
You'll never find a love so true.

But you had a life before me
That I could never share
Your loyalties and memories
Were with us everywhere.

Some people can forget the past
And live for something new
Some people can forget the past
But that's something you can't do.

Anne Seddon

SECRET TEARS OF CLOWN

You hardly ever notice me
No matter what I do
You just don't seem to realise
I think the world of you.

You seem so warm and gentle
So honest and so fair
And yet you just don't notice
How very much I care.

You mostly dance with just one girl
Nobody else you see
You'll never know how much I wish
That lucky girl was me.

I laugh and joke and carry on
To hide my breaking heart
It seems a shame you'll never know
I've loved you from the start.

I hope she'll make you happy
And never let you down
Meanwhile I'll carry on and be
The ever smiling clown.

Anne Seddon

MISSING YOU

I lie awake in bed each night
Reliving all my fears
Remembering the good and bad
The laughter and the tears.

I move my arm out hopefully
And find an empty space
My days I fill quite easily
It's night time I can't face.

I wonder what you're doing
Every minute of the day
I wonder if you're lonely
Since the day I went away?

Why could you not be happy
With the years we had ahead
Why let the past get hold of us
And break us up instead?

Maybe one day you'll understand
Just why I had to go
But I never will forget you
Because I love you so.

Anne Seddon

WHERE?

Where have all the years gone?
They have simply flown away.
Where have all my dreams gone?
They lessen every day.

Where have all my hopes gone?
They do not seem so real.
Where has all my laughter gone?
Only emptiness I feel.

Why does everyone I love
Either break my heart or die?
Why can I find no happiness?
No matter how I try.

Anne Seddon

WHEREVER YOU GO

No matter what becomes of you
No matter where you go
There's something that is very true
Yes, something you should know.

You may have been loved in the past
And in the future too
But there's only one love that will last
That's the love I have for you.

So darling please remember
Whatever you may do
No one will ever love you
The way that I love you!

No matter where life takes you
No matter where you go
One thing you must remember
Is that I love you so.

So darling please be happy
Wherever you may go
I wish you all the very best
Because I love you so.

Anne Seddon

GOOD ENOUGH

Good enough to cook for you
And wash your dishes too
Good enough to care for you
When you have the flu.

Good enough to do the bop
And take out dining too
Good enough in bed to hop
And to clean the flipping loo.

Good enough to live with
And share your daily strife
Yes! Good enough for everything
Except to be your wife.

My heart it breaks in pieces
I can hardly stand the pain
For even if you lost me
Your thoughts would be the same.

Because you'll never ask me
One thing you'll never know
Would my answer have been '*Yes*'
Or would it have been '*No*'

Anne Seddon

MY AUNT AND UNCLE

I have an Aunt and Uncle
Who've been so good to me.
I've had a lot of love from them
Through all my life you see

Throughout my life I've turned to them
No matter what went wrong
And with their love and guidance
I faced what came along.

They have no children of their own
To give their wisdom to,
So they have shared it all around
And given it to quite a few.

They are my rock, my strong support
Without them I'd be lost
They help and love and give their time
And never count the cost.

So 'Thank you Lord' for sending them
Into my life you see!
I love them so, I always will
For they mean the world to me!

Anne Seddon

MY FRIEND

I didn't know how old you were
The day that we first met
I only know a friend like you
Is very hard to get

I know you're apprehensive
As you reach the seven o
In fact instead of being glad
You're feeling rather low

Your age is not important
To those who really care
The only thing that matters
Is that you're always there

It doesn't really matter
If you're young or if you're old
The only thing that matters is
You have a heart of gold

So keep your chin up friend of mine
And have a lovely time
Because to everyone who is your friend
You make the whole world shine

Just wrote this poem to tell you
How very much I care
I hope you have a lovely time
I just wish I could be there!

Anne Seddon

THE COTTAGE

There is a cottage in the country
Where I would love to be
And the man who lives there in it
Means all the world to me

There is a cottage in the country
Along a bumpy track
A cottage that I had to leave
To which I never can go back

Living there was peaceful
So tranquil and serene
The countryside was beautiful
The river wide and clean

You walk out of the tiny garden
And down a little way
Into a secret garden
Where children love to play

Are the man and the cottage lonely?
Now that I've gone away
How I wonder if they miss me
As I miss them every day.

Anne Seddon

NIGHT OWLS

If you need someone to help you through a
Long and lonely night
Then tune in to Alan's 'Night Owls' and you will be alright

For he is there to help you and listen to your fears
He always understands your needs
And he'll chase away the tears.

The 'Night Owls' are special people
They are there to be your friend
They cheer you up and help you and your problems try to mend

So come on everybody! Tune in and you will find
The 'Night Owls' they are friendly
And honest true and kind.

Anne Seddon

I MUST TRY HARDER!

I must try harder to smile my way through life
To push completely out of mind
The toil and fears and strife
To count all of my blessings
And no more to be sad
And think of all the good things
To keep me feeling glad.

Anne Seddon

GOODBYE

At last I've had the strength to say
Goodbye to all the pain
At last I've had the sense to say
'You can't come back again'

And even though I love you
And even though I cry
I'm glad I had the sense to say
That very last goodbye

We fell in love so easily
I gave you all my heart
I really thought our love would last
And that we'd never part

One thing I never dreamed of
One thing I never knew
Was that you'd let your family
Come right between us two

How could you let this happen?
How could you let us part?
When the only thing I ever did
Was to love you from the start

How could you ever stand aside?
And let them hurt me so
How could you stand there quietly
When *they* said I had to go.

Anne Seddon

I hope you have been able to identify with some
of the feelings within this book.
I do not claim to be a proficient poet
But these poems come directly from the heart
And from my experience of life.

Anne Seddon